Mackenzie King and the Atlantic Triangle

MACKENZIE KING AND THE

ATLANTIC TRIANGLE

The 1976 Joanne Goodman Lectures
Delivered at the University of Western Ontario

By C. P. STACEY
Late University Professor,
University of Toronto

Macmillan of Canada / Maclean-Hunter Press

Canadian Cataloguing in Publication Data

Stacey, Charles P., 1906–
    Mackenzie King and the Atlantic triangle

(The Joanne Goodman lectures; 1976)

Includes bibliographical references.
ISBN 0-7705-1486-3

1. King, William Lyon Mackenzie, 1874-1950.
2. Prime ministers – Canada – Biography. 3. Canada –
Foreign relations – 1918-1945 – Addresses, essays,
lectures.* I. Title.

FC581.K5S73   971.06′22′0924   C77-001065-2
F1033.K53S73

Printed in Canada for
The Macmillan Company of Canada Limited
70 Bond Street
Toronto, Ontario
M5B 1X3

CONTENTS

THE JOANNE GOODMAN LECTURE SERIES
has been established by Joanne's family and friends
to perpetuate the memory of her blithe spirit,
her quest for knowledge, and the rewarding years
she spent at the University of Western Ontario.

FOREWORD

"They are chipping ice off the hotel like a frigate in
the North Atlantic," Colonel Charles Stacey an-
nounced as he arrived at the University of Western
Ontario on March 3, 1976 to deliver the first Joanne
Goodman Lectures. An ice-storm in the night had
plunged the city into crystal darkness, but, fortu-
nately, heat and light were restored to the Social
Science Centre before the lecture began. Despite the
weather, large audiences attended the lectures on
three successive days. An even greater audience
caught a glimpse of the lectures through the wide
press coverage they attracted. Those who were there
will welcome this volume as a tangible reminder of a
memorable occasion, while those who had to be
content with tantalizing snippets will now be able to
read the entire text of the lectures.

The Joanne Goodman Lectures have been
established at the University of Western Ontario to
honour the memory of Joanne Goodman, a second-
year history student at the university who died in a
highway accident in April, 1975. At the first lecture,
the Chancellor, the Honourable John P. Robarts, and
the Vice-Chancellor and President, D. Carlton
Williams, expressed the thanks of the entire univer-

sity to her parents, Mr. and Mrs. Edwin A.
Goodman of Toronto, her family, and her friends
for their generosity in choosing to endow a lecture
series as a living memorial.

Under the terms of the trust, each year a
prominent historian will be invited to the University
of Western Ontario to deliver three public lectures
on some aspect of the history of the English-
speaking peoples. The series will concentrate princi-
pally on the North Atlantic Triangle: Canada, the
United Kingdom, and the United States. These
annual lectures will play an important part in the
intellectual life of the university and, in their
published form, provide a major contribution to the
international world of historical scholarship and
literature.

It would have been difficult to find a more
suitable person as the first Joanne Goodman Lecturer
than Charles Stacey, Canada's most distinguished
military historian. Born in Toronto, he was educated
in the three countries of the Atlantic Triangle: at the
universities of Toronto, Oxford, and Princeton,
where he taught from 1934 to 1940. From 1940 to
1945 he was Historical Officer at the Canadian
Military Headquarters in London and subsequently
Director of the Historical Section of the General
Staff in Ottawa until he retired from the army in
1959. From 1959 to 1976 he was a member of the
History Department at the University of Toronto,
during which time he became University Professor
and a Fellow of Massey College. He is an Officer of
the Order of Canada and the Order of the British
Empire; a Fellow of the Royal Society of Canada;
the recipient of the Governor-General's Award and
the Royal Society's Tyrrell Medal; and the holder of

Foreword

several honorary degrees from Canadian universities. In a dozen books — most notably *Canada and
the British Army, 1846-71; The Canadian Army,
1939-45; Quebec, 1759; Arms, Men and Governments;*
and *The Arts of War and Peace, 1914-45* — he has
written on the military and diplomatic history of the
North Atlantic Triangle. Most recently, in *A Very
Double Life,* he has turned to an examination of the
private life of Mackenzie King, the major Canadian
politician for much of the first half of the twentieth
century.

By combining Mackenzie King and the Atlantic
Triangle in these lectures, Charles Stacey has
provided a distillation of his reflections on the
interaction of that extraordinary personality with
the events and leading political figures in Canada,
Britain, and the United States from the First World
War to the Cold War. His prose conveys the drama
and fun of the lectures which those who were
present will never forget.

Neville Thompson
The University of Western Ontario,
August, 1976.

PREFACE

When the University of Western Ontario kindly
invited me to deliver the first Joanne Goodman
Lectures in March 1976, it was explained to me that
Mr. Edwin A. Goodman desired that the lectures
given under the auspices of his endowment should
focus on the history of the English-speaking peoples
and particularly on the "North Atlantic Triangle". I
suggested that I might deal with the "Triangle" in
what Canadians have come to think of as the
Mackenzie King era. I did this because for the last
few years I had been living among Mackenzie King's
records to the point where I almost found myself
calling him what his few intimates called him while
he was alive — namely, Rex.

During the past few years William Lyon
Mackenzie King, long regarded as one of the dullest
dogs in Canadian history, has become, rather
suddenly, an interesting character. He achieved this,
long after his death, by a very simple means: the
diary which he kept for fifty-seven years. It is an
extraordinary document, comparable in scope and
interest with the journals kept by William Ewart
Gladstone in the nineteenth century and James
Boswell in the eighteenth. (There are many

the record of it is to be found in his voluminous papers and above all in his diary.

I take the opportunity to mention one point about King here. In one of my lectures I interpolated the remark that King was not a man of first-class intellect, or words to that effect. I based this assessment mainly on some of the accompaniments of his spiritualism — not on the mere fact of his being a spiritualist, for many able people have been spiritualists, but on such absurdities, recorded in his diary of the 1930s, as his belief that the secrets of the future could be discovered with the aid of tea leaves. To my astonishment, this remark, not quite accurately reported I think, turned up in newspapers across the country. I was even more astonished when supposedly intelligent people told me that it was absurd to suggest that a man of second-class intellect could have been Prime Minister of Canada for twenty-one years. When, in my subsequently published book, *A Very Double Life,* I ventured to speculate as to whether the University of Toronto perhaps showed sounder judgement than Harvard in the 1890s when the former refused King a graduate fellowship and the latter gave him the best it had, some people seemed disposed to scoff. I have, however, seen no reason to think that my suggestion was altogether ridiculous.

That Mackenzie King was a man of extraordinary political shrewdness is undoubted; but that is a different thing from first-rate intellect, the sort of intellect that graduate schools hope to find among their students (the operative word, as they say, is "hope"). My study of King convinces me that in his vigorous youth his mental equipment consisted of a respectable degree of general intelligence combined

with a remarkably retentive memory and a great
capacity for detailed work. That, I think, was all; but
it is, of course, a good deal more than many
Canadian politicians have had to help them on their
way. King recorded in his diary an incident during
his career as a student at Harvard that is revealing.
On November 15, 1897, he recovered a test paper
from Professor W. J. Ashley (afterwards Sir William), the noted economic historian who had
migrated from Toronto to Harvard in 1892 and was
later to return to his native England. Ashley had
given King the highest mark in the class — certainly
no indication of stupidity — an A-minus. (It must
have been a lean year.) But Ashley remarked that
although King had reproduced his lectures very
intelligently, "I gave an A against my rule never to
mark *unoriginal* work, because the reproduct'n is *so*
intelligent. But I do so with hesitation." It was
probably as good a comment on King's intellect as
anyone ever penned; and I am very much afraid that
King never altogether forgave Ashley for it, any
more than he forgave James Mavor, Ashley's
successor at Toronto, for denying him that
fellowship.

I must thank three people who have helped me
to prepare these lectures for publication: Barbara
Wilson, Jerry O'Brien, and Craig Brown.

C. P. S.
Massey College in the University of Toronto,
August, 1976.

Mackenzie King and the Atlantic Triangle

I. MACKENZIE KING'S
PERSONAL ATLANTIC TRIANGLE

I think I first became seriously aware of the North Atlantic Triangle — a phrase my old friend and teacher Bartlet Brebner had not yet made current coin — when I was a student at Oxford in 1927–29.

I had been brought up in Toronto on a diet of Queenston Heights and Lundy's Lane and the United Empire Loyalists, and I considered myself quite admirably anti-American. But I know now that that anti-Americanism of my youth was really a rather pale thing. We did not seriously expect hordes of bluecoats to come boiling across the Niagara River. The only invasion we anticipated was that of American industry, and we felt that it should be encouraged. Whenever a new American branch-plant opened in Canada we considered it a diplomatic victory; our government's policy, we told ourselves, was working well, and jobs were being created for Canadians. There was always a saving grace of humour about Canadian–American relations. People told the story of the census-taker who asked the Canadian farmer how many sons he had living. The farmer replied, "I got two living and one in the States." And there seemed to be few Canadian families that *didn't* have some member in the United States.

When I went to England in 1927 I encountered
real anti-Americanism, with nothing remotely funny
about it. Those were the days when the war-debt
question was poisoning the relations of Britain and
the United States. I recall Harold Innis watching the
passing scene from one of those little chairs they
used to rent in Hyde Park and saying sourly: "There
are only two sports in this country — gambling and
running down the States." One met bitterness and
resentment on every side. One day the president of
my college invited me to lunch. The conversation (as
always, it seemed) got on to the United States, and
as almost always it became rather intemperate. At
this point something happened to me that had never
happened before: to my utter amazement, I found
myself defending the Americans. (I realize now that I
was having a humble go at being a linch-pin.) My
effort was not very successful, for an English lady
guest at once terminated that portion of the
conversation by saying forcibly, "Oh, they're
horrible people; let's not talk about them."

Many things have changed since those days, and
since the later day when Brebner published his study
of "the interplay of Canada, the United States and
Great Britain". I can imagine some people criticizing
Mr. Goodman for setting up in 1975 a lectureship
focussed on "the history of the English-speaking
peoples and particularly on the North Atlantic
Triangle". I think there is some tendency today to
regard our Commonwealth relations as an irrelevant
relic of our colonial past. I also get the impression
that some people consider that the Americans are too
unclean to deserve study, even on the basis of the old
military principle of knowing your enemy. My own
notion is that we should do everything we can to

maintain and develop what is left of our Commonwealth connections, if only to provide some slight
make-weight against the overwhelming cultural
pressure of our North American neighbour. *That* is a
problem which no one can fail to recognize. But it
seems to me that there has never been a time when
the calm and intelligent and sympathetic study of the
United States and its relations with Canada was as
important to this country as it is now. I think it will
be a very poor day for Canada when any substantial
proportion of her people subscribe to the sentiments
of that stupid Englishwoman whose words, nearly
half a century ago, I remember so clearly.

However, I am not, thank God, a political
scientist. Our concern here is with history, and no
one can doubt the importance of the North Atlantic
Triangle in Canadian history, least of all in the era of
Mackenzie King.

For better or for worse, Mackenzie King was
one of the most thoroughly Canadian of our prime
ministers. His roots in the country were deep, and
his devotion to the memory of his maternal
grandfather constituted a special tie. When he was
arguing with the Minister of Finance about his
civil-service salary in 1902 he referred to "my love
for Canada inspired by grandfather's life & work".[1]
Very often he affirmed his belief that God had given
him the mission of carrying on his grandfather's
work, though his conception of the precise nature of
that work varied from time to time according to
circumstances. But it is worth remembering, along
with his Canadianism, that he was also one of the
most travelled of prime ministers. He visited China
long before China-visiting became fashionable. In
fact, he went around the world, at public expense, in

1908–9. A decade earlier he had spent the better part of a year in Europe on a Harvard travelling fellowship.

Like many Canadians, however, he was best acquainted with the other two countries of the Triangle. From 1896, when he left Toronto to study at the University of Chicago, until his retirement from office in 1948, there was probably never a year when he didn't spend some time in the United States, pursuing business or pleasure or a combination of the two. His visits to Britain were only less frequent. His personal connections with these two communities may, perhaps, be worth examining.

When King went to Harvard in 1897 it was the beginning of a lifelong love-affair. Harvard took him in and gave him everything, and King, I fear, never forgot the contrast with the University of Toronto, which had refused him a graduate fellowship. Long afterwards, when collecting, at Columbia, one of his innumerable honorary degrees, he wrote in his diary: "I owe very, very much to Universities of the U.S., more in many respects than to my own Alma Mater — most of all to Harvard."[2] When he visited New York he stayed at the Harvard Club, and got great pleasure from doing so. It was at the Harvard Club that King revised the draft of the Hyde Park Declaration with Clifford Clark and E. P. Taylor on April 20, 1941, before presenting it to President Roosevelt that afternoon. He wrote: "I immensely enjoyed working with these two men in the Harvard Club, in the quiet of that dignified splendid room."[3] Let me quote also what he wrote about the signing of the United Nations Charter at San Francisco in 1945: "I used the pen with the Harvard shield with my initials on it — a gift, some

years ago, from Joan [Patteson], though purchased
by myself at her request at the Harvard Club in New
York. This link with Harvard gave me very great
pleasure. There was something most fitting about
using this particular pen on this occasion, linking
Cambridge, Mass., with San Francisco, Calif. — a
sort of wider circle outside the political one from
Vancouver to Saint John."[4] King is being a bit misty
as well as mystical here, but he seems to be trying to
tell us that he feels himself a citizen of a community
larger — though not, I think, indefinitely larger —
than the country that elected him. At the very
moment when Brebner is inventing the North
Atlantic Triangle, King gives us another geopolitical
figure: "a sort of wider circle".

King had good reasons for being grateful to
Harvard. No other Canadian prime minister has
ever possessed the connections with American big
business and big money that King came to have, and
Harvard helped set his feet on that road. He earned
money by tutoring, and two of the students he
tutored were sons of the enormously wealthy Gerry
family. They invited him to stay with them at
Newport in the summer of 1899. It was an Arcadian
adventure with the idle rich. King denounced their
habits and customs in his diary, but it is pretty clear
that he was having a marvellous time all the same. It
is one of the curious ambivalences in King's life that
the friend of the poor, the disciple of Toynbee and
Jane Addams, should fall under the spell of the
American plutocracy; and yet I think this is exactly
what happened. He never lost touch with his
wealthy Harvard friends, and the circle of his
acquaintance among rich Americans steadily wid-
ened.

Take note of what happened later when King decided to look for a wife. This search went on sporadically from the time when he was a member of the Laurier cabinet until he became leader of the Liberal party in 1919. King knew plenty of women in Ottawa and Toronto — the reader of his diary soon discovers that every day was Ladies' Day with King — but he had no intention of marrying the girl next door. He looked briefly at a Miss Howard in Montreal, whom research reveals as a granddaughter of Lord Strathcona; but when that attachment languished he headed south. New York, Chicago, and Cleveland were the places where he carried on the hunt. Clearly, he wanted money, and he knew where the money was. In justice to King, however, we must add that he had not forgotten the poor. It is quite evident that he would not consider any woman who did not possess money, or, failing money, social position; but he also insisted that she should possess a social conscience. These may seem somewhat difficult specifications to meet; but King had a formula. He was an admirer of Dr. Wilfred Grenfell, the "Labrador Doctor", and an extraordinary number of the ladies whom he reconnoitred had connections with the Grenfell Mission. This, presumably, he regarded as a guarantee of high social ideals. (Perhaps he even remembered that Lord Strathcona was a prime benefactor of the Grenfell enterprise.) The one woman (so far as I know) to whom King actually proposed marriage in his mature years was Jean Greer (her family called her Daisy), a daughter of the Protestant Episcopal Bishop of New York. This was in 1918. She was a "noble and beautiful Christian woman"; she was active in "church and philanthropic work"; she occupied a high place in society; and though her family were not wealthy, they weren't poor either. King reflected, "She would make a true & perhaps a great man of me." There was only one obstacle. It is clear that many women were attracted by Mackenzie King, but Miss Greer, unfortunately, was not one of them. Next year she married a professor of music.[5] At the end of his long search for a wife among the best people in the United States, Mackenzie King remained a bachelor.

Thirty-one long years later, King, quite by accident, looked at his diary for 1918 and read what he had written about Daisy Greer. His comment was, "There is a case of a door closing, all to one's advantage . . . . Had I married her as I evidently had been prepared to do* I wd have become in all probability a citizen of the U.S. in association with large interests, not PM of Canada fulfilling my grandfather's life."[6] These musings remind one that in 1918–19 King was at a turning point. Though he had not succeeded in finding a wife in the United States, he had had enormous success there in another direction: that of the "large interests".

Everybody knows that shortly before the outbreak of war in 1914 King accepted an appointment as head of the Department of Industrial Relations in the Rockefeller Foundation. This brought him into a close relationship with John D. Rockefeller, Jr., and they remained warm friends until King's death. After the United States entered the war, King found himself in great demand as an

---

*This seems extraordinary — most men, I suspect, remember the women they propose to; but King, at this time, was a very old man.

industrial-relations counsellor to some of the country's biggest corporations. When he was criticized afterwards in Canada for allegedly failing to do his bit in the war, he was able to argue in Parliament that preventing strikes in American factories was a solid contribution to the war effort.[7] He did not mention that it was also extraordinarily lucrative. In November 1918, he recorded with satisfaction that he was making a cool $1,000 a week,[8] a great deal more than he made later as Prime Minister of Canada.

At the end of the war King's reputation in the American business community was clearly enormous. It is reflected in the fact that in 1919 he had the choice of continuing in the Rockefeller Foundation or becoming Director of the Carnegie Corporation, the remuneration in both cases being princely. He put aside both these rather glittering possibilities in favour of a return to Canadian politics.

What moved him to this momentous decision? It cannot be doubted that ambition played a part: King could be a bigger toad in the Canadian puddle than he could ever hope to be in the American pond. (After all, the American constitution bars a foreign-born citizen from becoming president.) And although in his earlier days King's ambition had pointed in other directions, he had long been infected with politics. Once that powerful virus enters the system, in most instances there seems to be no hope of recovery. King's was almost certainly a hopeless case. How far pure patriotism entered into his decision it is hard to say. I think it is clear that in King patriotism was closely bound up with family history. One recalls again that phrase "my love for Canada inspired by grandfather's life & work." God called him to carry on his grandfather's mission, and that, presumably, involved returning to Canada — it is difficult to resist the will of God. However, King certainly could have convinced himself that God meant him to marry the daughter of the Bishop of New York. And in that case, he might also have convinced himself that he could carry on Mackenzie's work just as well in the United States. Perhaps he might have ended up in the American Senate. It occurs to me that the Conservative Party of Canada has reason to regret that Daisy turned him down.

It is not an unfair assumption that King would not have chosen to go back to Canadian politics but for the likelihood of achieving the leadership of the Liberal party and, thereafter, the goal he had told his mother he had before him as early as 1901 — the office of Prime Minister. These objectives he duly reached, in 1919 and 1921. During the war, though he never gave up his Canadian domicile, he had spent a great deal of time in the United States. Naturally, this stopped when he became party leader, as, of course, did his work for American corporations. But he maintained his personal connections south of the border — that with the Rockefellers was probably the most important — and he continued to make frequent visits there. Back in 1908 he had written: "What appals one in New York is the haste and distraction of the place, the love of excitement, and the false standards of life."[9] He had overcome this aversion now, and a trip to New York was always a treat. In 1928 he acquired a new personal tie there, his warm friendship with Mrs. Beatrix Henderson Robb, a New York divorcée whom he met that year in Europe. I think it is probably true that after that year he never visited

New York without seeing Mrs. Robb. After he
finally became a spiritualist in 1932 he visited at least
one medium in New York. He never found there,
however, quite the satisfaction he experienced in the
spiritualistic community in Great Britain.[10] Generally speaking, when King found time for a short
vacation, it was towards the United States that he
turned. In this, of course, he was merely a typical
Canadian of his time and class.

I leave aside for the moment the era of Franklin
Roosevelt and the Second World War, on which I
shall have a good deal to say later.

It is quite obvious that there was a good deal of
ammunition ready to hand for those King-haters
(and King-haters were always numerous) who
regarded Mackenzie King as disloyal both to Canada
and the Empire and an American at heart. But there
is another side to the story which the King-haters
did not know about, and which they would not have
publicized if they had.

King first visited England on that Harvard
fellowship in 1899. The social historian will be
interested to note that the London prostitutes
tempted him, and he fell, just as he had fallen earlier
in Toronto and Chicago and Boston. (The accepted
image of King changes a bit as one reads the diary.)
On the political side, we observe that the South
African War was just breaking out, and that the
young man was not immune to the imperial
enthusiasms of the day. When he hears of Canadian
troops leaving for the Cape, he writes: "I had a hard
time to restrain my feelings as I read of the liberality
& grt. enthusiasm of our people at home. If England
knew as much of & cared for Canada as Canada does
for her there wd be a strong sentiment. Yet I find the

feeling for Canada strong wherever I go, &
Englishmen seem glad to welcome me as a
Canadian." He shared the current sentimentality
about the old Queen. When, in 1901, the news came
that she was dying, King wrote, "We have all loved
her, we will all ever be proud of having lived while
she was Queen."[11] That he lived while she was
Queen is indeed a point worth remembering. (He
was almost exactly the same age as Winston
Churchill.) Few people ever succeed in completely
living down their origins. King's origins sometimes
got rather heavily overlaid with other matter; but
the student of his career should never forget that he
was an Ontarian and a Victorian. Of course, he was
also the grandson of the rebel William Lyon
Mackenzie; but he never admitted that Mackenzie
could justly be called disloyal or anti-British.

   If King was fond of New York, it is equally true
that he was fond of London. There, as in New York,
he had dear friends. One of them was Violet
Markham, whom he first met when she visited
Ottawa in 1905. She was rich and generous, and she
helped King financially on a number of occasions.
One might have thought that Violet would have
been the ideal wife for King, for she had lots of
money and oodles of social conscience. King,
however, just does not seem to have thought of her
that way. Perhaps his mind was absolutely set on a
female American plutocrat. Nevertheless, he and
Violet were intimate friends for forty-five years. At
a somewhat later time he formed a rather similar
friendship with the painter Frank Salisbury and his
wife Maude. These were probably his closest
personal friendships in England. Spiritualism
brought him other connections, and I fear King had

enough snobbery in his makeup to be pleased that some of them were with the very best people — the old Marchioness of Aberdeen, the Duchess of Hamilton, and Viscountess Grey of Fallodon. With people he knew well he was as much at ease in England as in the United States. If it was a question of casual acquaintance, like many Canadians he found some Englishmen heavy going. The famous phrase "an air of effortless superiority" keeps turning up in his diary in one form or another, often in connection with the little English enclave at Government House in Ottawa.

What were Mackenzie King's real inner feelings about Britain and the United States and their relationship to Canada? We are seeking here, I suppose, the quintessential King. And where, if anywhere, is the quintessential King to be found? Doubtless, if the answers exist, they are to be found in that colossal compilation, the diary. I venture to suggest, very tentatively, that the diary may offer a special source of personal revelation about King that has not yet been tapped.

In November 1933 King was introduced, apparently by the Dominion Archivist, Dr. Arthur Doughty, to the spiritualistic procedure known as table-rapping (King spelled it *wrapping*). He was already accustomed to seek contact with the unseen world by séances with a medium. Now he found himself able to engage in what may be called "do-it-yourself" spiritualism, in which he and his friend Mrs. Patteson conversed over the table with the spirits of the departed without the assistance of any third party. It is my impression that rapping soon gave place to a more direct form of communication in which King acted, in effect, as a medium

himself, receiving messages and repeating them
aloud for the benefit of Mrs. Patteson. Whether this
is true or not, between 1933 and the outbreak of war
in 1939, and in some cases later, King and Mrs.
Patteson held large numbers of informal séances
over the table, in which they believed they had
contact with dead members of their families and
with other people in the "beyond." King recorded
these conversations in pencilled memoranda, apparently written while the séance was in progress.
Usually, they are to be found attached to the original
diary.[12]

Anyone is, of course, at liberty to believe that
these were genuine conversations with the other
world. My own opinion is that they came straight
out of King's subconscious mind. If I am right in
this, then it seems to me possible that in these
memoranda of séances we are coming pretty close to
what I have called the quintessential King. These
sessions were strictly private. Apart from King
himself, no one knew of them except the utterly
loyal and discreet Joan Patteson. Here, if anywhere, I
think, we can look into King's inner mind and catch
glimpses of his fundamental ideas, if that is the right
word.

Let me give an example that is relevant to our
present business. The date is December 17, 1934:
King's sixtieth birthday. All birthdays were important to him, but this one was, of course, particularly
so. And "the little table" (as King always called it)
played a great part in the celebration.[13] He wrote in
the diary: "Between 9:45 and 10:45 Joan and I had an
hour with the little table. It was beautiful, the
manner in which one after the other of the loved
ones "came trouping [*sic*] in", and how the number

included the Leaders of Liberalism in the old land
and this . . . ." The families were out in force; even
King's paternal grandfather, Bombardier King of the
Royal Artillery, was among those present. (He
didn't often make it.) Then there were the personal
friends, and among these were the Lauriers. It was
natural that it should fall to Peter Larkin to introduce
the contingent from overseas (after all, he *had* been
High Commissioner). Here is King's description:

> Then passing to the old world. Love from London
> — the great political leaders: Grey of Falloden [*sic*]
> whom I dearly loved, Lord Oxford, Gladstone,
> McLean [Sir Donald MacLean], Roseberry [*sic*]—
> Campbell-Bannerman — a marvellous group. Then
> the Canadian Liberal Leaders, Alexander Macken-
> zie, Edward Blake & "the whole lot of us" — a
> typical political expression. Then 'try to speak to
> Toronto's first Mayor' — How beautifully as-
> sociating . . . with the [Toronto] Centennial celebra-
> tion and linking grandfather with my present &
> future, giving him the joy of saying what is to come
> [Mackenzie had said "You will be Prime Minister
> next year"] — how rejoiced he must be to see this
> vindication of his life & work — the Prime
> Ministership — my part to draw England & Canada
> closer together — a marvellous completion of his
> aims & work — The grandson of the one whom [*sic*]
> the Tories said was "disloyal" seeking to save &
> secure the British Empire as the greatest agency of
> peace & good-will in secular affairs . . . .

Apart from what it tells us about King's ego,
two things interest me about this birthday celebration. The remarkable group of eminent people who

assembled to do honour to King that evening were
all British or Canadian. The absence of Americans is
rather striking. One might have expected President
Theodore Roosevelt, whom King had known, to
appear and offer a word of greeting. It would not
surprise one if President Lincoln had joined the
roster — he had, in fact, spoken to King at least once
over the table, in company with Laurier and
Gladstone.[14] But no, this very special birthday party
was a purely British Empire affair; and I cannot help
feeling that this may have some significance. Of
course, it is possible that the omission of Americans
was due to the fact that the United States did not
possess a Liberal party; for the other point that
strikes one is that this was a Liberal occasion.
Disraeli didn't come; Sir John A. Macdonald didn't
come. But the Liberals were there in numbers,
standing behind their boy. When the long line of
notables had been introduced and had duly offered
their love, King asked, "Will you all help me this
year? Please." The reference was clearly to the
coming election, and the reply, apparently from
Larkin, was, "We will help all we can." (What
chance had R. B. Bennett? The Angels of Mons
weren't in it.)

At this point I find myself asking just what did
the terms Liberal and Conservative, or Grit and
Tory, mean to Mackenzie King? He was a supremely
successful operator in the field of practical politics,
but he was no political theorist. His diary indicates
to me that his notions about the basis of parties were
few, simple, and fixed. It is clear that he thought of a
British Conservative as a man who believed in
centralizing the Empire, and who spent a good deal
of time plotting to that end. Canadian Conserva-

tives, in King's book, accepted and encouraged this attitude. Liberals in both countries opposed it and were therefore autonomists. Moreover, a Liberal was *ipso facto* a friend of the people (like William Lyon Mackenzie), whereas a Conservative was a tool of the Big Interests (like the Family Compact). I think it is fairly evident that King really believed this. It is clear too that he saw an essential consanguinity between the Liberal parties in Britain and Canada, and also between the Conservative parties in the two countries: the party of Laurier and Blake was also the party of Gladstone and Asquith. In this King was merely following an old Canadian tradition, for Macdonald had certainly felt that there was a kinship between his party and Disraeli's, and a gulf between his party and Gladstone's.

At the same time, I think it is the case that in King's political science there were strong elements of the atavistic and of the purely personal. Historically, a Tory was to him the sort of person who had opposed (King would have said, persecuted) his grandfather; in his own time, Tories were the sort of people who had undermined Sir Wilfrid Laurier and who failed to be attracted by the idea of Mackenzie King being Prime Minister of Canada forever. King had, I think, mentally adopted Laurier into the King family immediately after Sir Wilfrid's death (though Laurier's unfortunate agnosticism seems to have resulted in his never being anything better than a second-class King).[15] Mackenzie and Laurier were his two inspirers, and, to some extent, were the standards by which he judged men and policies. After 1933, of course, King was in constant touch with both of them over the little table, and they gave him, not as a rule political advice, for that he seldom felt he needed, but moral support and confidence to comfort his chronic insecurity.

King's attitude towards the English Liberals was influenced not only by ingrained and inherited prejudices, but also by personal contacts made during his two visits to England in 1908, and especially, probably, the second one. He arrived in London that December a newly elected Canadian MP, conscious of his dignity, clearly with a tremendous chip on his shoulder, prepared to be patronized, if not actually insulted, and to make himself unpleasant accordingly. But the members of H. H. Asquith's Cabinet, and two of them in particular, treated him with marked consideration. Lord Morley asked him to Christmas dinner, and they had a long and elevated conversation which King recorded in detail. Still more important, the Foreign Secretary, Sir Edward Grey (who never came to London if he could help it) invited the young Canadian to stay overnight at Fallodon, his country house. They discussed foreign affairs and also the nature of true greatness; and King wrote afterwards: "Everything considered, it was, perhaps, the most remarkable conversation I shall ever have with any man . . . . It is hard to describe the simplicity and beauty of his nature . . . ."[16] As a result of this visit King became Grey's devoted admirer for life.

King's reactions to the outbreak of war in 1914 are worth noting. At the end of July he was in Ottawa, making himself visible in a manner calculated to let no one forget that, though momentarily out of Parliament, he was one of the leaders of his party. Though he was disposed initially to think that Germany's action in the crisis was excused by the hasty Russian mobilization, it never occurred to him to oppose Canadian participation in the war that might come. He thought it vital that the Canadian Liberal leaders should be together in Ottawa "in a position to present a united front with the Conservatives & have a policy. We must stand by Britain solidly & unitedly, if she is not the aggressor which she will not be with the men now at the head of affairs." His first thought was that the English Liberals would prevent Britain from being drawn in: "I cannot believe knowing Asquith, Grey & [Viscount] Haldane to be the men they are war will come with Germany. Winston Churchill is the one dangerous factor . . . . The security of England & the Empire lies with Sir Edward Grey, Asquith & Haldane, above all with Grey." On the other hand, "If the other party were in power war with Germany wd. be a certainty. They take the position now is the time to destroy German power, that is what the Tories at the Rideau Club are all saying." (Note that a Tory was a Tory, whether he lived in London or Ottawa.) But when the situation changed, and Grey made his famous speech on August 3, emphasizing the German violation of Belgian neutrality and the British obligations to defend it, King, like untold millions of other people, accepted the implication. The speech was, he said, "a noble, dignified & righteous utterance".[17] One is left feeling that for Mackenzie King the First World War was a good war, or at least an acceptable war, because it was a Liberal war and, more specifically, Edward Grey's war.

A terrible thing, however, was about to happen. Disrupted by the war, the British Liberal party ceased to be a dominant force in political life;

whereas the Canadian Liberals, under King's assiduous nursing, recovered from their own disasters of the war period and were able to control the future. It is interesting to speculate what the result would have been if the British Liberals had had a better fate and had been a governing party between the wars. I cannot help feeling that political relations between Canada and Britain would have been rather different from what they actually were. King's superstitious regard for the word "Liberal" would have operated as a lubricant which was not present in his dealings with Conservative ministries in London; and though it is likely that the ultimate result, so far as the constitution of the Commonwealth was concerned, would have been much the same, it might have been achieved with rather less abrasion of feelings.

How is one to define Mackenzie King's attitudes towards the English? I think it is clear that he did not dislike Englishmen as such. It is equally clear, however, that he did dislike Tories, in England as in Canada. The warm friendships he formed in England tended to be limited to Liberal circles. Subject to this qualification, I think it fair to say that King's feelings for the English were those of a good Victorian and a good colonial. (It is worth remembering that many good Victorian colonials combined a deep theoretical regard for *England* with a strong distaste for many *Englishmen*.)

I come back to the séances over the little table. King's sixtieth birthday party is really quite representative. On great occasions he tended to call in eminent Britons to give him counsel and support. Early in 1935, at one of the few moments when he asked for political advice, he sought it from Lord Oxford as well as from Laurier. A week before the

election of 1935, Gladstone, Lord Morley, Lord
Oxford, and Lord Grey all spoke of King in the
highest terms, as did Laurier and members of the
King family, to say nothing of St. Luke and St. John.
(Were *they* Liberals too?) The night before the
election, Gladstone, Oxford, and Grey were back
again, and Grey told King that though he, Grey, had
failed to end war, King would succeed. The total
absence of Americans continues to be marked.[18] It
seems apparent to me that King had a yearning for
the approval of eminent Englishmen — provided, of
course, they were Liberals.

If, as I tend to believe, King's meticulous
records of his sessions with the little table are a
revelation of his inner mind, those Canadians who
accused him of being an American at heart were far
off the mark. He liked Americans, as most Canadians did and do. If they were wealthy and important, he liked them that much better. But they were
not part of the inner circle; that was reserved for
subjects of the King. (Incidentally, King George V
himself talked to King and Mrs. Patteson over the
little table in connection with the abdication crisis
and the royal visit of 1939.) In the last period of
King's life, there was, of course, one American who
was an exception to all rules: Franklin D. Roosevelt.
When King was going the rounds of the London
mediums in 1947 and 1948, Roosevelt pretty well
monopolized the séances. (One of his advantages
was that he had made himself solid with the Prime
Minister's mother in the next world; she called him
Frank.[19] It is hard to imagine any other American
achieving that particular distinction.)

I mentioned the monarchy. We have seen King
paying his tribute to Queen Victoria, and, generally

speaking, he gave the same respect to her successors.
The royal family, of course, could hardly expect to
be on quite the same level as the King family. In
1934, as already noted, King watched with interest
the celebration of the centenary of Toronto's
incorporation as a city, never forgetting that his
grandfather was the first mayor. A high point of the
occasion was a famous public altercation between
the 1934 mayor (W. J. Stewart) and the governor
general (Lord Bessborough) on the front steps of the
City Hall. King's comment was: "A century hence
there will be no King or his representative &
Mackenzie's name will be honoured above that of
sovereigns & their representatives by the people &
the city."[20] As a general rule, however, though he
had his doubts about many of the sovereign's
representatives, the sovereign himself commanded
King's regard. His vanity was flattered when, as
prime minister, he was brought into close contact
with royalty; and, increasingly, he seems to have
come to the conclusion that royalty were really quite
nice people. When he attended Princess Elizabeth's
wedding in 1947, he observed that the reception at
the Palace was "much more dignified, quiet and
natural than most weddings that I have attended";
and his final word was: "One felt what a marvellous
family the royal family really is."[21]

I am left with the strong impression that, in
spite of all Mackenzie King's American contacts and
connections, he was in essence a Victorian Canadian
from Ontario, whose inherited values were British,
and who admired British ways, coveted British
approval, and was devoted to the British connection.
If I am right in this, how does it happen that he is
remembered as a cranky autonomist who sup-

posedly took a leading part in dismantling the
British Empire? And how did it happen that he was
so cordially and universally disliked in government
circles in Britain? People in Whitehall would have
roared with laughter at the thought of King
receiving "Love from London" as a present on his
birthday. Yet to King this seemed the most natural
thing in the world. It is doubtful whether he ever
realized just how much concentrated hostility had
accumulated to his account in the old capital of the
Empire.

This situation is both comic and tragic. I shall
try to illuminate it a little in my next lecture.

II. THE HERMIT KINGDOM, 1921–30

In his Rhodes Memorial Lectures of 1926, published later under the title *Canada in the Commonwealth,* Sir Robert Borden said: "We beyond the seas must remember that each nation stands at the threshold of every other, that all frontiers touch one another throughout the world, that there can be no hermit nation and no hermit continent."[1]

This was the language of the future. These sentiments were to be common form after mankind had suffered through a second world war, but they were not the popular language of the 1920s. When Borden spoke, Canada's great neighbour in North America, as he was only too well aware, was busily engaged in trying to prove that it was both desirable and possible to be in very fact a "hermit" nation, insulated from the sort of dangerous entanglements that had involved the United States in Europe in 1917. The same tendencies appeared in Great Britain, and one suspects that if that country had had as much water between it and Europe as the United States had, the British would have been at least as isolationist as the Americans.

Mackenzie King became Prime Minister of Canada at the end of 1921. I suggested in my last lecture that King's fundamental nature was British, colonial, and Victorian. If he had been leader of a country with a homogeneous population and no recent history of internal difficulties, these tendencies in him might have had free rein; but this was not the way things were in 1921. The events of 1917–18 centring on conscription had disastrously alienated French Canada. The French were one-third of the Canadian population; and it so happened that it was on that particular one-third that King's political power largely depended. He had written when he heard of Sir Wilfrid Laurier's death, "Quebec dominates the House of Commons."[2] It was mainly Quebec votes that made him leader of his party in 1919, and he could never afford to forget the solid phalanx of sixty-five Liberals that Quebec had sent to the Commons to support him in 1921. But Quebec's mood was grimly isolationist. What is more, Quebec was not alone in this, since throughout the country there was war-weariness and disillusionment. American attitudes had, as always, considerable influence north of the border. If King's policies were isolationist, it is arguable that they simply had to be.

There is no evidence that King regretted this. He probably would have rejected the phrase "a hermit nation" as a description of his concept of Canada. (He knew that memorable phrases could be embarassing, and I think he consciously preferred forgettable ones — it was not King who thought up the famous words "a fireproof house".) In practice, however, the Canada of Mackenzie King's conception in 1921 was not, I think, too different from that of a happy hermit viewing the world from a comfortable cell, equipped with all modern conveniences.

So far as I know, King never put on paper a
comprehensive statement of his goals at the moment
when he took office. He had carefully refrained from
issuing a "manifesto" during the campaign (he
explained long afterwards that Sir William Mulock
had once told him that manifestos were just targets
for your enemies to shoot at.)[3] But the record of his
government shows us doors closed, adventures
rejected, and expenses cut. The old slogan of English
radical liberalism, "peace, retrenchment and re-
form", would have fitted King's government quite
well, if only he had been a little more of a reformer.
Add to this Sir Wilfrid Laurier's repudiation of the
"school which wants to bring Canada into the
vortex of militarism which is the curse and the blight
of Europe",[4] and you have a fair representation of
King's policy (almost anything Laurier had ever said
was all right with King). And I repeat that it seems
quite evident that these old principles were fully
acceptable to the majority of the Canadian people in
1921.

I should like to look briefly at the question of how
external policy was formed under King. This is
relevant to our subject, for external policy in King's
time consisted almost entirely of policy towards
Britain and the United States.

When people think of external policy under
King, they tend to think of O. D. Skelton, the
fugitive from Queen's University who was Under
Secretary of State for External Affairs from 1925
until his death in 1941, and who is quite properly
thought of as the most powerful civil servant in
Canadian history. Perhaps, however, they think of
Skelton rather too much. King was making policy

by himself for quite a long time before Skelton joined him. Skelton appears, in a temporary capacity, only in 1923, and makes the final break with Queen's only in 1925. Before that, King was literally a one-man Department of External Affairs. He refused to make use of the able Loring Christie, who had done such important work under Borden and Meighen, because he thought he was a Tory; and finally he froze Christie out of the service (though King, who could convince himself of almost anything, seems to have convinced himself later in life that he had offered Christie the under-secretaryship before it was given to Skelton).[5] He drafted his own dispatches to London, in addition to doing all the work of the office of prime minister; and the record indicates to me that quite a few of the difficulties with London after 1921 were due to King's deficiencies as a draftsman, and particularly to his talent for circumlocution and obfuscation. I think it is evident that the broad lines of King's external policies were quite clear before Skelton joined him, and indeed before King took office. Skelton gave them a sharpness and clarity they had not had before, and he relieved King of the day-to-day routine of drafting papers; but he was not the author of King's system of external policy.

There were some striking differences in the two men's attitudes. Long afterwards, Vincent Massey said bluntly that Skelton was anti-British.[6] Massey was perhaps too pro-British himself to be a really good witness on this point. Nevertheless, my reading of the records convinces me that he was right. And there is evidence from a better witness than Massey: namely, Mackenzie King himself. In 1929 King complains in his diary that Skelton has been "putting one over" on him, by removing from dispatches the phrase "diplomatic unity of the Empire". To Skelton that phrase was anathema; to King it was, let us say, not quite anathema. A little later, we find King saying, "Skelton is at heart against the Br[itish] Empire, which I am not. I believe in the larger whole, with complete independence of the parts united by cooperation in all common ends." During the final descent into the Second World War, we find King being quite severe about Skelton: "I felt his negative viewpoint and inferiority complex in so many things — a real antagonism towards monarchial institutions, and Britain, a sort of communist sympathy — lack of larger view in reference to world affairs — an isolated Canada — which I cannot accept."[7]

One might ask, if King sometimes felt this way about Skelton, why did he keep him around? The answer is quite simple: he couldn't do without him. Skelton was so competent and so industrious that he became indispensable to King as soon as he joined him. He certainly influenced King in many things, and they very frequently saw eye to eye. It was Skelton who set the tone of the growing Department of External Affairs between the wars. That tone was determinedly isolationist, and it did not change with changing circumstances as the second war came on. By 1939, students of public affairs were aware that the Department of External Affairs was utterly out of touch with the mood of the country.

If Skelton mistrusted British influences on Canadian life, I think it is fair to say that he would have welcomed more American influence and worked to that end. Back in 1902, when working in

the United States, he wrote to Adam Shortt,
wondering, as he said, "whether the ideal I've
always cherished, Canadian independence, is fated to
be only an ideal". He went on to rail at "the policy of
those who believe they can afford to neglect the U.S.
as a factor in Canada's future, pile up tariff barriers &
deepen national prejudices in a vain attempt to
deflect the current of destiny, and who believe there
can be any real or lasting community of interest
between Canada and Australia or Timbuctoo, or
whatever other part of the map a Jingoistic spree
may chance to paint red."[8] Here we have a glimpse
of Skelton's mind, and though the date is very early
it does not seem to have changed greatly in later
years. The Skelton this letter shows us is an extreme
nationalist who dislikes Canada's British connections and much prefers those with the United States.
Much other evidence points the same way.

One thing a hermit nation apparently did not need
was *defence*. This was King's very strongly held
view, and one gets the impression that the vast
majority of Canadians in the 1920s agreed with him.
Who, after all, was the country going to fight?
Certainly not the United States. Laurier had pro-
claimed that long ago; and King, knowing the
Americans as he did, certainly never gave a
moment's thought to the possibility of war with
them. Here again, after 1918, almost all Canadians
were with him. I don't believe King ever heard of
Defence Scheme No. 1, the incomplete draft plan for
action in case of an American war which various
writers have had fun with in recent years. I am sure
that if he had he would have been profoundly
shocked. Skelton probably did not know of it until

1931, and in that year the scheme was cancelled. It had been an essentially dead duck since General McNaughton became Chief of the General Staff two years before, and indeed it had never been a very live duck.[9]

As for wars abroad, Canada had helped beat the Kaiser and lost 60,000 men in the process. We had a League of Nations now, and people hoped it would work: perhaps there would never be another world war. If there was, perhaps we could keep out of it. Virtually nobody except the officers of the tiny Canadian fighting services drew from the experience of 1914–18 the moral that the country should maintain a higher level of preparedness than before the war. In this respect the contrast with the situation after 1945 is interesting.

King himself was one of the most unmilitary products of an unmilitary society. Hating war, he also hated the military services. In 1920, as Leader of the Opposition, he visited Victoria and had a look at the naval establishments at Esquimalt. He wrote, "The whole institution with the 'Rainbow' at the wharf seemed a great waste of public money. Idle officers, 15 mounted police, etc. It is shameful the waste on these military & naval fads . . . ."[10] Fifteen months later, as prime minister, he was able to do something about such "waste", and he set to it with glee. It is true that the defeated Unionist government had really left him very little to do. When an extremely modest naval program was produced early in 1920, there was a violent revolt in the Unionist caucus, which very nearly caused the total abolition of the navy.[11] The country's military expenditure, which had been nearly $400 million for the last year of the war, was down to below $31

million in 1920–21. King, however, did even better.
He slashed and slashed, until by the beginning of
1923 he was almost sympathizing with the Minister
of National Defence. "I felt sorry for him as we
pressed for further reductions, he almost cried under
the strain of his reductions of staff, etc." In 1924–25
the expenditure was down to about $13 million.[12]
Later, under the influence of prosperity, the Liberals
relented a little. In 1928 we find King actually
approving some naval construction,but on a special
basis: "At Council I put thro' the order for 2
Destroyers to be built *in England*. Not a word was
said when I read the order through. I thanked
colleagues for deferring to my wish not to have [the]
name of [the] Administration identified with
creation of a 'war industry' in Canada."[13] War
industries were clearly immoral. A time would
come, all the same, when those industries would be
very respectable, and King would be exerting
himself actively with his colleagues to encourage
war production in Canada.[14]

It is time to consider specifically King's attitudes in
the twenties towards the two other points of the
North Atlantic Triangle — those two countries,
Britain and the United States, both of which he
knew so well and with both of which he had ties of
personal affection and regard.

    The relationship with Britain took up far more
of King's attention than did dealings with the United
States, and it has taken up more space in the history
books. I do not propose to rehash the whole story of
the conferences of 1923 and 1926 and the advance of
Dominion autonomy which issued in the end, while
King was in the political wilderness, in the Statute of

Westminster of 1931. I must, however, make a few generalizations about it.

I remarked in the beginning that King did not dislike Englishmen as such, but that he did dislike Tories. He had enormous respect for certain English politicians, but the ones he respected were all Liberals. Unfortunately, the English Liberal party had now disintegrated, and when King came to power Britain was ruled by the Lloyd George coalition. King did not like the Lloyd George coalition. I suspect that he had never regarded Lloyd George as a true Liberal. In 1914, when, as I remarked earlier, the personnel of the Asquith ministry gave King the confidence that enabled him to support the war, Asquith, Haldane, and, above all, Grey were the men who impressed him; Churchill was "the one dangerous factor"; Lloyd George he did not mention. It is possible that Lloyd George was later damaged in King's eyes by his association with the Canadian Tories in the Imperial War Cabinet and at the Peace Conference. The dangerous Churchill was Colonial Secretary when King became Prime Minister of Canada. King undoubtedly regarded the coalition as Tory in all but name.

The outlook was bleak for Anglo-Canadian relations if Canada's prime minister could only be easy with a Liberal government in England; for there was never going to be a Liberal government again. However, there was Labour; and King was apparently prepared to regard Labour with a tolerant eye — as merely Liberals in a hurry. When Ramsay MacDonald formed his first Labour government in January 1924, King wrote that it was "on the whole better I believe than any since days of Asquith's", and added, "I wish him well."[15] Not many weeks later, however, King was at odds with MacDonald over the latter's statements about the Lausanne Treaty. One feels that no true Liberal would have done what MacDonald did.

King's dislike of the Lloyd George government is part of the background of the famous Chanak Affair of 1922. I probably don't need to remind this audience of how the British government — and primarily Lloyd George, Churchill, and Birkenhead — faced with the advance of Turkish nationalist forces towards the Dardanelles, invited the Dominions to associate themselves with British military preparations and to send contingents. It was an ill-considered action taken in the worst possible way; for a statement to the press telling what was in the message to the Dominions reached the Canadian newspapers before the message itself reached the prime minister. King's reaction to Lloyd George's message was characteristic: "It is drafted designedly to play the imperial game, to test out centralization vs. autonomy as regards European wars."[16] In other words, it was a plot. So far as the Dominions were concerned, this was pretty clearly untrue. A plot involves some process of connected thought, and there certainly wasn't much thinking done before the approach to the Dominions. If there was a plot — and many people in England, including Stanley Baldwin, a member of the coalition ministry, thought there was — its object was to foment a war with Turkey to enable Lloyd George to win an election. The whole affair reeks of irresponsibility.

The tragedy of Chanak is that it tended to confirm Mackenzie King's suspicions of English Tories and their centralizing practices. And the whole business played into King's hands as he

approached the question of the relationship of the
Dominions to British foreign policy. The immediate
issue was dealt with when King's government told
Lloyd George that Canadian public opinion would
require consultation with Parliament before a
contingent was sent. The larger question awaited the
Imperial Conference of 1923.

The governments of Borden and Meighen had
pursued a nationalistic external policy; but its
nationalism had consisted in their demanding a share
in the formulation of the policies of the Empire.
Their conception was that the Empire — which
some were beginning to call the Commonwealth —
should have a common foreign policy, but that that
policy should be arrived at by consultation between
Britain and the Dominions. This concept had
emerged from the deliberations of the Imperial War
Cabinet of 1917–18 and the British Empire Delegation at the Peace Conference. It had been acted upon
by the Imperial Conference of 1921; but the serious
confrontation that took place in that meeting
between Canada and Australia over the renewal of
the Anglo-Japanese Alliance suggested what a very
difficult scheme it was going to be to work in
practice.

At the Conference of 1923 Mackenzie King
challenged this idea of a common Empire foreign
policy and, essentially, destroyed it. Aided and
supported by an able and passionate paper by
Skelton, who accompanied him to the conference as
an adviser, he made no difficulty about reversing the
policies followed by Canadian governments for a
decade past — his version and Skelton's was that
those policies were themselves a reversal of Canadian tradition and an aberration. The King–Skelton

formula was that each country of the Commonwealth should have its own foreign policy and
conduct it in accordance with its own interests. At
the same time, they admitted that there were issues
of fundamental concern to the whole Empire: "With
these all parts of the Empire must deal; the
Governments of the Empire must confer; the
Parliaments of the Empire, if need be, must decide."
The conference made no formal repudiation of the
common-policy idea; neither, however, did it
reaffirm it, or make any provision for carrying it
into effect. In retrospect, it is clear that King won a
complete victory. In doing so he put an end to what
Loring Christie called the "project of co-operative
unified diplomacy" of which Sir Robert Borden had
such high hopes.[17]

Borden and his associates had seen Canada as
part of a world community, part-proprietor, so to
speak, of a world power, the British Commonwealth, and exercising, as she did at Paris through
the British Empire Delegation, at least a degree of
influence on the great power's policy. The degree, of
course, was limited, and Skelton's complaint was
that the system involved for the Dominions "a
maximum of responsibility and a minimum of
control". When the arrangements were being made
for the Paris Conference, Borden had been afraid
that Canada would end up being treated like "Siam
or Hedjaz".[18] Presumably, King and Skelton did not
think precisely in terms of placing Canada in the
same category with those countries, but their plan
certainly involved accepting the status of a small
independent state. Under it Canada would have the
influence that would come naturally to a country of
nine million people; that, and no more. One seems

to come back to the happy hermit in his cell.

Nevertheless, I sometimes think that the most significant thing King said at the Imperial Conference of 1923 was not his repudiation of the Borden–Christie concept of Commonwealth co-operation, but a rather passing and casual comment upon the influence of the United States on Canadian opinion. It was important, he said, but it might be overruled. "If a great and clear call of duty comes, Canada will respond, whether or no the United States responds, as she did in 1914, but it is a most important consideration against intervention in lesser issues."[19] King was saying that a Chanak was one thing, but a world war, threatening the existence of the Empire, was quite another. I feel sure that he never changed his opinion that in such a crisis it would be quite impossible for Canada to stand aside. It should be added, of course, that this was an opinion he refrained from broadcasting. The proceedings of the Imperial Conference were highly confidential.

Few of the people who heard King make this remark in 1923, I imagine, recognized its importance, though it may well have sent a cold shiver down the back of O. D. Skelton. The conference undoubtedly left many people in London disliking Mackenzie King intensely. His determined autonomism, and, in particular, his evident intention that Canada was to pursue an independent foreign policy in matters which she considered exclusively her own business, were greatly resented. The foreign policy objective had been made amply clear in the Halibut Treaty affair earlier in the year, when King insisted that that agreement with the United States should be signed by a Canadian representative only, without participation by the British ambassador in Washington. The fact that King behaved with such unvarying politeness during the Conference probably didn't help much; and even that could scarcely be said for his performance in connection with the Halibut Treaty.[20] Of that, however, I shall say something more in a moment. The thing that probably seemed strangest and least defensible to many Englishmen was the fact that King coolly and deliberately reversed the attitudes taken by Canada in a succession of earlier conferences. The British representatives probably did not take as seriously as they should have King's remark during a discussion on naval defence "that those of us who differed from the centralising point of view should not be regarded as less the friends of a permanent imperial relationship than those who are using high sounding phrases".[21] I suspect that King's image in London did not begin to improve until after 1930. When the British found themselves dealing with R. B. Bennett, many of them, I am sure, wished that Mackenzie King was back.

As a result of the 1923 Conference, however, King established at least one valuable new contact in London. The new British prime minister, Stanley Baldwin, talked to him with what Baldwin called "appalling frankness". This is King's account of what Baldwin said about Chanak: "England and the Empire were in the hands of three dangerous men, all intoxicated with their own cleverness and love of power, and prepared to sacrifice everything to it; foolish and blind even to the point of believing that they could win an election by bringing on another war. They were determined to have war with Turkey and were doing everything in their power to

bring it about . . . ." Baldwin also told King (so King
reports) that Canada's action in the Chanak crisis
had been "entirely proper" and that it had "helped to
save the day".[22] It is not surprising that King
thought well of Baldwin, even though he was so
unfortunate as to be a Tory.

In 1927 Baldwin came to Canada as part of a
British delegation to take part in the celebration of
the sixtieth anniversary of Confederation; also
included were two royal princes. King was on such
good terms with the Baldwins that, knowing that
Mrs. Baldwin had an interest in the occult, he
arranged that she should have an interview with his
tame fortune-teller from Kingston, Mrs. Bleaney,
the nearest thing to a medium he had at that stage in
his psychic development. Unfortunately, the ladies'
conversation does not seem to have been very
productive.[23]

King found the party from England very
anti-American. (I recall that this was the period of
my own experience in England, of which I have
spoken.) The only person he reported as not sharing
the hatred of the Americans was the Prince of Wales;
and he, unfortunately, behaved badly in other
respects. Baldwin asked King to let "his fertile
mind" work on the problem of what should be done
if the royal family "should 'throw up' a sort of
George IV".[24] It was to be nine years before that
matter finally came to a head.

During these discussions in 1927 King sought to
perform the ancient, traditional, and perhaps largely
mythical function of the Canadian as the interpreter
between Britain and the United States. Just after the
British party's arrival, he writes, "I tried to lessen
B[aldwin]'s bitterness against the U.S." As they

prepared for the opening of the Peace Bridge at Fort
Erie, King had a bright idea: "I . . . asked what he wd
think of my proposing a treaty of Perpetual Peace —
between U.S. and Grt. Br. — Go the Americans one
better on their disarmament scheme." But Baldwin
"thought that wd would require much consideration
— did not seem to favour the idea." So King
abandoned it.[25]

This is a good point at which to say something about
King's policies towards the United States in his early
years as prime minister.

    In those years after 1921 there was really not a
great deal of important business going on between
Canada and the United States. With Britain, we have
seen, there was the great question of constitutional
relations. But what can one hermit kingdom say to
another hermit kingdom? There were endless
matters of small day-to-day routine, but of large
policy discussion there was very little. The one great
problem that eclipses all others in Canadian-American relations is always trade; but when King came
to power there was nothing to be done about that.
The Republicans were now in control of the
executive and the legislature in Washington. Their
first act was to repeal the low tariff of the Wilson era,
replacing it first with an emergency measure at
much higher rates, and then with the Fordney-
McCumber tariff, the highest the country had yet
had. The Canadian Liberal platform of 1919 had paid
lip-service to the Reciprocity arrangement of 1911,
and had voiced the hope that a "favourable
moment" might come when the two governments
would be prepared to revert to that policy. Clearly,
the early twenties were not that favourable moment.

In any case, Mackenzie King, I suspect, was disinclined to start monkeying with the tariff. Reciprocity had had an adverse effect on his own career, and I am sure he had not forgotten it. In January 1911, when the Laurier Cabinet was discussing the measure, he "spoke out strongly about the danger to Ont. of interfering much with mffrs., said that certainly I for one wd. not be returned if we did. . . ."[26] The measure really did not "interfere much with manufacturers", but the member for North Waterloo duly lost his seat. Tariff changes during King's first two administrations were limited to a certain amount of tinkering designed to please the West. For major measures King was quite content to wait for the favourable moment. That moment was to come, but not for many years.

Nevertheless, I think it is clear that King, at the beginning of his ministry, was determined to make a *beau geste* to the United States. After all, he knew the United States better than most people, and he certainly considered himself exceptionally qualified to conduct relations with it. Moreover, Washington evidently had a place in his plan to establish relations with London on a new footing: it was natural for him to inaugurate his independent Canadian foreign policy in the American capital.

So it was that in July 1922, some eight months after he was sworn in as prime minister, and just after the end of his first parliamentary session in that office, Mackenzie King set off for Washington. This episode is curiously obscure. A major reason for this is that King, with less than his usual regard for history, had let his diary lapse. Lacking his report of

the events and his explanation for his actions, we are
driven back on the newspapers, and on speculation.
King's authorized biographer, Dawson, makes no
reference to this Washington trip.

It seems pretty evident, however, that King
consciously designed this foray as a diplomatic
mission, intended to inform the United States
government that on matters of purely Canadian and
American concern the Prime Minister of Canada
proposed to deal with them direct, and to inform the
British government that in such matters Canada did
not require the assistance of British diplomatic
officers and did not propose to act through British
channels. A diplomatic mission, however, must have
a subject. Trade, we have seen, was hardly a
practicable topic. The St. Lawrence Seaway was in
the air, but the government was not ready to act on
it. King evidently looked about him and selected, of
all things, the Rush–Bagot Agreement limiting
naval armaments on the lakes.

The original exchange of notes between Britain
and the United States back in 1817 was still in effect,
but its details had been rendered obsolete by changes
in naval architecture. The Canadian naval service
had been mildly exercised over the fact that the
Americans were actually maintaining on the lakes
more armed vessels — chiefly revenue cutters —
than the letter of the agreement allowed. King
himself seems to have felt that the agreement's worst
inadequacy was the fact that it was subject to
cancellation on six months' notice by either party.
He is quoted as saying that this meant that it lacked
"that element of certainty and permanence which is
all-important with respect to matters pertaining to
defense".[27] The issue was clearly neither important

nor pressing, but it gave King the necessary excuse for his mission to Washington. It is worth remarking also that it clearly appealed to a romantic and sentimental ingredient in King's attitude to the United States. It is to be remembered that before 1914 he had been deeply involved in the plan for a celebration of the century of peace between the Empire and the Republic. In precisely the same class, of course, was his suggestion to Baldwin of a "treaty of Perpetual Peace". It seems quite possible that "romantic and sentimental" may have been Baldwin's mental comment on that short-lived project.

In view of the nature of the business to be done, King was accompanied to Washington by George P. Graham, the Minister of Defence. On July 12, they called at the State Department and, we learn from the press, "at a conference with Secretary of State Hughes they proposed that the ideals of the Rush-Bagot agreement . . . be perpetuated in a new treaty between this country and Canada". Hughes was reported to be "highly sympathetic and interested", but only the "general purpose and spirit" of the plan were discussed. King told the Toronto *Globe,* "We feel that here is an opportunity for Canada and America to give a lesson in international good-will and friendly dealings." That afternoon, King and Graham were received at the White House by President Harding. The next day, they visited the U. S. Senate and were entertained at dinner by Senator Gerry of Rhode Island, whom King had tutored in his Harvard days and who was one of the boys who had invited him to Newport in 1899. They seem to have dined with the British *chargé d'affaires,* who was also present at the luncheon

tendered them by the Secretary of State; in general
however, the British element was very much in the
background.[28]

One imagines that King returned to Ottawa
with a comfortable sense of "mission accom-
plished". The unproductive negotiations which
followed are interesting, I think, chiefly for one
detail that has escaped notice. Hughes had asked for
a draft treaty. The Canadian naval staff prepared
one, in consultation with Loring Christie, whose
services King seems to have made use of on this
occasion only. King sent the draft to Lloyd George
with a request for British comments.[29] He explained
that there was no idea that the American ships on the
lakes represented "any unfriendly intention", adding
that "their presence however, if it became realized
might arouse unfortunate recriminations and mis-
understandings in the minds of the Canadian people
who have valued so highly the arrangement of 1817,
and it would be deplorable if the situation were
allowed to precipitate demands for counterarming
on our part." He described his visit to Washington,
remarking: "Our reception at the hands of the
President and the Secretary of State was satisfactory
in every way." Of the proposed treaty King said that
while it primarily concerned Canada, it undoubtedly
also affected "in some degree the political relations
of the Empire towards a great Foreign Power", and
the original agreement had been made with the
United States by Great Britain; therefore, he asked
for the views of the British government, and
particularly for any technical suggestions.
His cable contained the following interesting
paragraph:

As for the method of signature of the proposed
Treaty our view is that, having regard to the
character and implications of the document, it
would be appropriate that the full powers should be
issued to Canadian subjects of His Majesty. When
the time comes therefore we propose to pass an
Order in Council authorizing the issue of full
powers to myself as Prime Minister and Secretary
for External Affairs and to my colleague, the
Minister of National Defence, to sign on behalf of
His Majesty.

In London, the Colonial Office duly noted the
implications of this: "The constitutional point
arising is whether the Treaty should be signed, on
the British side, *only* by Canadian plenipoten-
tiaries."[30] However, the Chanak crisis exploded a
few weeks later and the constitutional point seems to
have got lost in the debris. The reply which the
British Prime Minister finally sent to King makes no
reference to the method of signing.[31] If, as appears to
be the case, the British government simply made no
comment on King's innovative suggestion, there is
considerably less reason for accusing King of
rudeness the following year, when he seemed to
"spring" on the British authorities the proposal for
an independent Canadian signature in the Halibut
case.
    The trip to Washington in July 1922 thus seems
to emerge as a preliminary sketch of Mackenzie
King's ideas and policy in Triangle diplomacy. We
have clearly presented here the idea of direct
negotiation by a Canadian cabinet minister or
ministers with the American authorities. This was
nothing very new, as Canadians had often carried

the burden of negotiation with Washington in commercial matters. Borden had undertaken personally an important mission to Washington in 1918.[32] Equally clear, and more novel, is King's intention that treaties primarily of interest only to the United States and Canada should be signed on the Canadian side without the participation of any British official. It is worth noting also that another of King's principles — consultation between the countries of the Commonwealth in matters of common concern — is not entirely absent from the affair. One more point may be worth making: all this happened in the first year of King's administration, long before the appearance of O. D. Skelton on the Ottawa scene.

I should note that nothing actually came of all the high-sounding talk about the Rush–Bagot Agreement. Canada duly forwarded a draft treaty to Washington (through the governor general and the British ambassador), and the U.S. government duly presented a counter-draft (not very different) through the same channel. Nothing more happened. The last item on the file is a polite inquiry from the State Department in 1925 as to when a reply from Canada may be expected.[33] It appears that no reply ever went forward. The Rush–Bagot Agreement had served King's purpose. It remained on the books, unamended, but constantly pointed to as a shining example of civilized behaviour in international affairs, until 1939, when, under greatly altered circumstances, the first of many modifications was readily arrived at.

The affair of 1922 brings something else to mind. It may seem curious that King was so very slow about appointing a Canadian minister to

Washington. He had inherited this project from
Borden, though he had insisted on repudiating the
part of the Borden plan that would have made the
Canadian minister the number two man in the
British embassy. The Canadian Legation, King was
determined, should be a completely separate entity.
In 1922 he asked Sir Arthur Currie whether he
would be interested in being minister; Currie said he
couldn't afford it.[34] No appointment was made until
1926–27, when the job went to Vincent Massey,
who could afford it. The whole thing was remarkably leisurely. One reason, I suggest, was that King
didn't think the appointment was very important
anyway. Neither the High Commissioner in London
nor the minister in Washington was a very vital
functionary in King's eyes, and he gave them little
significant work to do. Here, the affair of 1922 again
indicates his preferences: when he had important
business with London, he sent a prime-minister-to-
prime-minister cable; when he had important
business in Washington, he got on the overnight
train and went to see the Secretary of State, or
preferably the President. The excursion of July 1922,
I suggest, prefigures the procedures of the 1930s and
1940s, the days of Franklin D. Roosevelt, when King
became a fairly familiar figure at the White House.
To those great days I shall address myself next.

III.   THE JUNIOR PARTNER, 1935–48

On the evening of October 13, 1935, an elderly
gentleman and a somewhat older lady sat hunched
over a table at 335 Laurier Avenue East in the city of
Ottawa. The man was Mackenzie King, who for five
years past had been Leader of the Opposition in the
Canadian Parliament, a post which he did not think
ideally suited to his capacities. The woman was his
friend Joan Patteson. They believed themselves to be
in contact with the spirit world.

This was a particularly important "sitting", for
on the following day the people of Canada were to
go to the polls in the country's eighteenth general
election since Confederation. King hoped, and
practically everyone expected, that they would reject
the government of R. B. Bennett and return himself
to power. The omens were favourable that night. Sir
Wilfrid Laurier, speaking through King's dead
father, assured him that he would win handsomely.
Although most of the other advance information
Laurier gave about the election turned out to be
inaccurate, on that main point he was right.[1] In ten
days King was back in the prime minister's office,
and thereafter he continued to rule Canada for
thirteen years, until his retirement in 1948.

During those years the western world was
dominated to an extraordinary extent by two great
personalities: Franklin D. Roosevelt and Winston
Churchill. The official relationships of Canada with
Britain and the United States in this period centred
in the dealings of Mackenzie King with these two
men, the American president and the British prime
minister. Those dealings were largely influenced by
the fact that Roosevelt and Churchill both enjoyed
enormous personal prestige with the people of
Canada at large.

King's personal relationship with Roosevelt
began almost precisely at the moment when King
returned to office. The Depression, which had
ruined Bennett's government as it had ruined King's
five years before, was the dominant fact of
contemporary political life. In the end, it had had a
chastening effect on economic policy in both
countries. In the United States, the Roosevelt
administration obtained from Congress in 1934 the
Reciprocal Trade Agreements Act which gave it a
largely free hand in negotiating reciprocity with
foreign countries. In Canada, Bennett, having failed
to cure the Depression by raising the tariff, was
anxious to obtain a trade agreement with the United
States before going to the country in 1935. The
administration in Washington, however, dragged its
feet, and Bennett lost the election, as he probably
would have done even if he had been able to wave a
trade treaty under the noses of the electorate.[2] This
was the situation when King became prime minister
for a third time; and he clearly felt that it offered him
a great opportunity.

It must be remembered that Franklin D.
Roosevelt was already enormously admired in

Canada, chiefly because of the vast vigour with
which he had attacked the problems of the economy.
At the same time, access to the American market
certainly seemed to a great number of Canadians the
best expedient in sight for pulling the country out of
the Depression. The fact is that in 1935 the
"favourable moment" for reciprocity, held up as a
hope for some future day in the Liberal platform of
1919, had at long last arrived: reciprocal trade was
not only acceptable to the Canadian public, it was a
popular goal. In these circumstances, King embraced
it with enthusiasm.

During the interval between the election and the
swearing-in of the new government, O. D. Skelton,
still Under Secretary of State for External Affairs,
had a frank talk with the American minister in
Ottawa, Norman Armour. Armour's account indicates that Skelton, no doubt cheered by the Liberal
victory, talked with unusual frankness. Armour
reports that Skelton said that Canada was faced with
a choice between developing closer relations with
the United States or closer union with the Empire.
Skelton, for both political and economic reasons,
preferred the States. As for King, he had hardly taken
the oath when he was beating on Armour's door. He
didn't wait for the minister to call on him; he called
on the minister, and did it on Thanksgiving Day.
Having resumed his contact with Skelton, he spoke
in much the same terms as Skelton had. Here is
Armour's report:

> . . . Mr. King stressed the great importance of a
> successful trade agreement at this time on the
> relations between our two countries. He made it
> clear, as Dr. Skelton had done, that there were two

roads open to Canada, but that he wanted to choose
"the American road" if we made it possible for him
to do so. From every point of view it was important
that our attachments should be strengthened and
our relations brought closer in every way, politically
as well as economically. So strongly did he feel on
this point that he even suggested that if I thought it
would be welcomed or would help the situation he
would be glad to consider proceeding himself to
Washington and having a talk with the President.

Armour tried to moderate King's enthusiasm. He
suggested that it was not certain that a trade
agreement was within immediate reach. However,
he underestimated King, and perhaps underestimated Roosevelt's interest in having an agreement
with Canada. On November 8, the Canadian prime
minister was in the White House, and the next day a
trade agreement was initialled (it was fortunate that
the Conservatives' abortive negotiations had laid the
groundwork). It was signed on November 15, little
more than three weeks after King had taken office.
He had dramatically demonstrated to the Canadian
people that his administration was on terms of close
confidence with the great leader in the White
House.[3] I think it cannot be doubted that he had
hitched his wagon to the Roosevelt star.

That first visit to the White House on
November 8 had gone well socially, quite apart from
its economic aspects. The president and the prime
minister remarked that they had met at least once
before* — at Harvard, when King was getting an

*The diary's phrase is "The President . . . asked if I recalled
the last time we had met." There is no reference to any
earlier meeting.

honorary degree and Roosevelt was a member of the Board of Overseers. This enabled the president, when proposing King George's health at dinner that night, to refer to the prime minister as "an old personal friend". Roosevelt talked about the family summer home at Campobello in New Brunswick; King and Mrs. Roosevelt talked about Jane Addams and Hull House. It really seems as though a fairly good time may have been had by all. "In saying goodnight, the President said it was great just to be able to pick up the telephone and talk to each other in just a few minutes. We must do that whenever occasion arises. I will always be glad to hear from you."[4] A new relationship was off and running.

I am not going to tell over again the story of how that relationship developed during the next few years. But I should at least recall that, as the threat of war grew, there was a visible tendency for the United States to interest itself in Canadian security. In 1938 Roosevelt actually came to Canada — a remarkable thing in itself, when one reflects that neither President Coolidge nor President Hoover had thought it worthwhile to return the visit which the governor general, Lord Willingdon, had paid to Washington in 1927; and he used the occasion to announce that the United States would not "stand idly by" if Canada were threatened. Roosevelt managed to give Canadians the impression that he was genuinely interested in and friendly to their country. No other president had ever done that. His popularity in Canada continued to grow. I have no doubt that he was far more popular with Canadians than Mackenzie King ever was.

The first result of the outbreak of war in 1939 was to interrupt the communications between the

president and the prime minister. King tactfully
respected the limitations which neutrality imposed
on Roosevelt. But as soon as the shooting war burst
out in the West, in the spring of 1940, the
relationship became active again. The fall of France
produced near-panic on both sides of the border.
Adolf Hitler was the chief architect of a *rapprochement*
between the United States and Canada whose symbol
was the Ogdensburg Declaration of August 1940.

About that famous affair I should like to make
just two points. First, note that although Americans
at the time and later assumed that the Ogdensburg
meeting was the result of a request from Mackenzie
King, this was not so. King knew better. He let
Roosevelt take the initiative. The second point is that
Ogdensburg was approved by virtually everybody
in Canada. The thing that apparently led Roosevelt
to pick up the phone and invite King to Ogdensburg
was a letter from the American minister in Ottawa
reporting that Canadians were demanding "some
form of defence understanding with the United
States". Mr. Moffat wrote, "The old fear that
cooperation with the United States would tend to
weaken Canada's ties with Great Britain has almost
entirely disappeared. Instead, Canada believes that
such cooperation would tend to bring Britain and
the United States closer together, rather than to
force Britain and Canada apart."[5] In the circumstances of that summer, "imperialists" and
nationalists alike favoured any measure that
brought the United States closer to the en-
dangered Commonwealth.

Had people been able to look into the future and
see Ogdensburg as a turning-point in the growth of
American influences on Canada, some of them

might have been less enthusiastic; yet so desperate was the crisis that many, I think, would have been prepared to pay the price. One contemporary observer who was not prepared to pay the price was Winston Churchill. He observed grumpily that there might be "two opinions" about some aspects of the Ogdensburg arrangement. No doubt he perceived that from that moment it was likely that American influence would increase faster in Canada, and British influence would decline. No doubt also he was displeased at not having been consulted.[6]

Thus we arrive at the question of King's relationship with Churchill. This is rather more complicated than the one with Roosevelt. The two men's paths had crossed on various occasions, and, generally speaking, it may be said that until the Second World War Mackenzie King disliked and distrusted Churchill. We have seen his low opinion of Winston as a member of the Asquith Cabinet of 1914. In 1922 Churchill was one of the prime movers in the Chanak Affair, a grave crime in King's eyes. Nevertheless, one discovers with surprise King speaking kindly of Churchill when the latter visits Ottawa in 1929. His unexpected comment was: "A fine mind, nice nature. . . . Have really much enjoyed his visit & society."[7] Ten years later, however, Mackenzie King, visiting the Roosevelts with the King and Queen, was glad to hear King George say that he would not wish to appoint Churchill to any office "unless it was absolutely necessary in time of war". The Canadian prime minister wrote in his diary, "I think Churchill is one of [the] most dangerous men I have ever known." But within a few months it *was* a time of war and Churchill was First Lord of the Admiralty; and King was listening to one of his broadcasts and wishing that he could speak like that.[8]

A few months more, and Churchill was prime minister of Great Britain. King certainly was not overjoyed. There is a somewhat comic contrast between the warm telegram that King sent to Neville Chamberlain, the fallen chief, and the restrained one that went to Churchill: "May you be given the vision and the endurance so necessary to the duties of your high office and never more needed in the guidance of public affairs than at this critical hour." At once, however, it became evident that Britain, the Commonwealth, and the Allied cause had found the leader that the times required. Churchill's appointment coincided with the loosing of the German *Blitzkrieg* in the West. On May 19, 1940, he made his first broadcast as prime minister. Next day, King cabled him that he had heard it "with feelings deeply stirred and with profound admiration and pride".[9] This, I have no doubt, was sincere; and King's feelings were shared by people around the world, including millions of Canadians. Suddenly the people of Canada had another hero to set beside Roosevelt; and this was something their own little prime minister had to learn to live with.

I think it is the case that King's regard for Churchill grew as time passed. The admiration was reluctant, but it was there. The final tribute was written in King's diary while he was in London in 1947: "I felt that perhaps in more respects than one, he was the greatest man of our times."[10]

King knew that he was at a great disadvantage by comparison with both Roosevelt and Churchill. He suffered from chronic insecurity; this, I am sure, was why he felt the need of support from the spirit world. He knew that, as an orator or as a personality, he was not in the same class with the two great men. He knew too that he was short and pudgy and, in general, physically insignificant. One of his private miseries throughout the war and afterwards was the unfortunate tendency of Canadians to refer to Churchill and Roosevelt as "our leaders" and to forget their genuine home-grown leader. The final blow came after the war when the offensive formula was indelibly engraved on some bells at Niagara.[11] King was sure that all this was the work of the Tories, but that didn't make him feel any better about it.

He knew, however, how this difficult situation could be made to serve his own purposes. If the people of Canada could be convinced that he, King, was a close and friendly associate of the two heroes, it would be a very great political advantage to him. Accordingly, he lost no opportunity of impressing the public with his familiarity with Churchill and Roosevelt. Here, he felt, was a weapon which, if properly used, would win him a general election any time. And in 1945 he did, in fact, use it in the campaign, urging the electorate not to disregard the "intimate and far-reaching associations" that had been formed between the men directing the nations and elect an administration of individuals who did not know the leaders of other countries.[12]

The question is inevitably asked, how close was King to Churchill and Roosevelt? How genuinely intimate were these friendships of which he made so much? Unfortunately, there is little evidence available except from King. Neither Churchill nor Roosevelt kept a diary like King's which could tell us what they really thought about him. They were both almost extravagantly polite to him, and I have seen nothing in his own diary to make me doubt Mike Pearson's suggestion that they managed him by playing up to his egoism.[13] And the diary leaves me believing that he never felt really close to either of them. Among other things, the question of names is interesting: they both called King "Mackenzie", and they were the only people who ever did. It seems they were not sufficiently interested or sufficiently intimate with him to find out what his friends called him. When Mary Pickford came to Ottawa in 1948, King told her his friends called him Rex, and thereafter they were Rex and Mary to each other.[14] He never ventured to do that with either Churchill or Roosevelt. When he called Roosevelt "Franklin", which he did only sometimes, he thought it important enough to note in the diary. If he ever called Churchill "Winston", I do not remember seeing the record of it.

If there was genuine friendship with either man, it was with Roosevelt rather than with Churchill. King and Roosevelt at least had Harvard in common. But the mask of affability that Roosevelt wore was presented to all the world, and nobody really knew what went on behind it. As for Churchill, his whole background and set of values were so different from King's that it is hard to believe that he had any warm feeling for "Mackenzie". He needed King's help, and he flattered him accordingly. But if he had thought of the Canadian as a real comrade there would not have been that curious incident when Mackenzie asked for some indication of the date of the Normandy D Day, and Winston told him that it might be as late as June 21. (The present generation may need to be told that the landings actually took place on the sixth.) If I may imitate a bad habit of King's and quote myself, this "might be uncharitably defined as an exercise in the art of how to deceive a Dominion prime minister without actually lying".[15]

This brings me to the question of Canada's relationship, or lack of it, to the higher direction of the war. It is now fairly well known that Canada had no share, or virtually none, in that direction, and that the Canadian government was sometimes not consulted even on special matters on which it clearly ought to have been — the Dieppe shackling being an example. It is also well known that Mackenzie King was unwilling to join battle with his great friends and allies on these questions. To quote Mike Pearson again, he normally "accepted the situation with a mild complaint or none at all".[16] That statement could be documented almost *ad infinitum*.

I limit myself to just one example, the story of the First Quebec Conference of August 1943. It is important and striking.

When it was first suggested that Churchill and Roosevelt and the Combined Chiefs of Staff should meet on Canadian soil, King was urged to insist on being given dignified status in the conference. (It will be remembered that the Combined Chiefs of Staff was a purely Anglo-American committee.) Norman Robertson, Skelton's successor as Under Secretary of State for External Affairs, argued, says King, "that if Churchill and Roosevelt met on Canadian soil, I would have to be with them as an equal. He did not see there was need of Canadian staff being associated with British and American staffs [how like the Department of External Affairs!] but felt the people of Canada would expect me to be in full conference with both Churchill and Roosevelt." King remarks, "I saw the force of this but felt embarrassment in the matter."

Malcolm MacDonald, the British High Commissioner, was present, and added his voice to Robertson's. If King thought it embarrassing to raise the question of his personal position, MacDonald could do it, "and make it quite clear that it would be a mistake to have the meeting at Quebec unless I were more than in the position merely of host to Churchill and Roosevelt. . . ." It is surely rather remarkable to find the British High Commissioner and the Under Secretary of State for External Affairs teaming up to urge the Prime Minister to take a strong national stand. However, their endeavour failed. King drafted a cable to Churchill including a paragraph "to the effect that the position of PM of Canada would necessarily have to be considered when the meeting was on Canadian soil." Subsequently, however, he decided to strike this out.[17] Even so, the cable as sent through MacDonald was evidently enough to inspire Churchill to attempt to make a place for Canada at the Conference. MacDonald, perhaps, had said a word on his own account.

Churchill now sent King a message saying that he expected no difficulty in arranging that King and the Canadian Chiefs of Staff should attend *plenary* meetings of the conference (he emphasized that the British and Americans would still be able to retire into private session). But when this proposal reached Roosevelt he met it with a resounding veto. If Canada was let in, he said, Brazil and China would immediately clamour for admission, not to mention Mexico and the other British Dominions. Evidently

anticipating some difficulty with King, Roosevelt
sent the Canadian ambassador in Washington,
Leighton McCarthy, post haste to Ottawa to explain
matters; he appears to have told McCarthy that he
would not come to Canada at all if Churchill's
dreadful plan were persisted in. The President need
not have worried. King recorded: "I told McCarthy
at once that I had never even suggested this proposal
but that it had come from Churchill himself,
Churchill evidently feeling he wished to meet our
wishes as far as possible. I said there would be no
difficulty on that score."[18] King's anxiety not to give
Roosevelt one moment's uneasiness is almost comic.

King's motives in this affair are, in fact, clear
enough. He was not interested in a share in
discussing strategy, about which he knew nothing.
He was interested in his image before the Canadian
people as the associate of the two great men — as
long as they were at Quebec, and he was at Quebec,
everything would be all right. He wrote privately:
"My own feeling is that Churchill and Roosevelt
being at Quebec, and myself acting as host, will be
quite sufficient to make clear that all three are in
conference together and will not only satisfy but will
please the Canadian feeling, and really be very
helpful to me personally."[19] And that was the way it
was. The British and the Americans met behind
closed doors at Quebec, and Canada provided the
whiskey and soda, and King had his picture taken,
many a time and oft, with Churchill and Roosevelt;
and General Maurice Pope, whose usual task was
picking up titbits of information for the Canadian
authorities around the offices of the Combined
Chiefs of Staff in Washington, came to Quebec and
did the same thing there.

I think it is evident that Mackenzie King's reluctance to press for a share in the direction of the war was at least partly rooted in politics. He considered that his friendly relationship with Churchill and Roosevelt was a great political advantage to him, and he was unwilling to disturb it by making demands which they might think embarrassing. In fairness to King, it should be remarked that even if he had tried harder it is quite unlikely that he could have acquired much influence for Canada in the councils of the alliance. One should also add that, from the point of view of military efficiency, it is very undesirable that the committees controlling the operations of a wartime coalition should become too large. What Canada could legitimately have hoped for was more attention in matters where her special interests were involved, and more formal recognition of her sovereignty as a fighting member of the group. An example may explain what I mean. When the Allies fighting the war in the Pacific drew up directives for Admiral Nimitz and General MacArthur, those directives were issued in the names of Great Britain, the United States, Australia, and New Zealand. When a directive was prepared for General Eisenhower covering the campaign in North-West Europe beginning in 1944, nobody even thought of mentioning Canada, although it will be recalled that quite a few Canadians fought in that affair.[20] That omission might not have taken place under a more pushing prime minister.

I might mention one other curious point. King more than once said, and apparently believed, that it was easier for Canada to get what she wanted from the Americans than from the British. I don't want to bother you with masses of evidence, but I can say

that everything I have found in the records points to
a precisely contrary conclusion. The story I just told
about the First Quebec Conference and the widely
differing attitudes of Churchill and Roosevelt is a
telling piece of evidence. Equally striking is the
question of the public announcement of Canadian
participation in the landings in Sicily in July 1943.
Those who read Colonel Nicholson's history will
discover that the obstacles to publication were, first,
General Eisenhower, who objected on security
grounds to mentioning the Canadians in the first
instance, in spite of pressure brought upon him on
our behalf by the British; and, secondly, somebody
in the War Department in Washington, who, after it
had been arranged that Mackenzie King would
announce Canadian participation twenty-four hours
after the landings, proceeded to scoop him by
publishing the news on D Day itself.[21] I still
remember the horror with which the staff at
Canadian Military Headquarters in London heard
that the Canadian prime minister had made a speech
in the House of Commons attributing the attempt to
keep the news from the Canadian people to "the
military authorities in Great Britain". CMHQ had
found those authorities both sympathetic and
helpful, and considered that they had done very well
by us. I don't believe King ever understood what
had really happened.

Against this apparent readiness to put the best
possible interpretation on American actions, and the
worst possible one on those of the British, one must
set something else. As the war went on, King
developed increasing suspicions of the Americans in
Canada, particularly in the North-West. In March
1943, Malcolm MacDonald (the only British High

Commissioner who was ever on terms of personal
friendship with King) was invited to report to the
Cabinet War Committee on the situation in the
North-West, which he had lately visited. He said, in
effect, that American activity there was getting out
of hand. The result was the appointment of a Special
Commissioner for Defence Projects in the North-
West, whose instructions made him responsible for
safeguarding Canadian sovereignty. A few months
earlier, in connection with a proposal for a joint
Canadian–American study of the lands opened up
by the Alaska Highway, King was worrying about
"efforts that would be made by the Americans to
control developments in our country after the war,
and to bring Canada out of the orbit of the British
Commonwealth of Nations into their own orbit".
He wrote, "I am strongly opposed to anything of the
kind. I want to see Canada continue to develop as a
nation, to be in time, as our country certainly will,
the greatest of nations of the British Commonwealth." He had doubts about the Canol project to
produce oil in Canada for American military needs.
He said in his diary: "With the United States so
powerful and her investments becoming greater in
Canada, we will have a great difficulty to hold our
own against pressure from the United States."[22]

During King's last months in office there was an
incident of great interest. A suggestion came from
Washington for what amounted to unrestricted
reciprocity. At first, King was prepared to buy it,
writing, "The country had learned they had made a
mistake in not accepting the treaty in Sir Wilfrid's
day." He told the Minister of Finance to go ahead
with it, but after a few weeks he began to have
doubts. He spoke of "my experience in Laurier's

Cabinet re reciprocity" (was he remembering how
the honourable member for North Waterloo had lost
his seat?) and "said I felt sure that the long objective
of the Americans was to control this Continent."
Finally, he had words with Mike Pearson: "While I
might miss [*sic*] to be the head of the Government, I
would never cease to be a Liberal or a British citizen
and if I thought there was a danger of Canada being
placed at the mercy of powerful financial interests in
the United States, and if that was being done by my
own party, I would get out and oppose them
openly." It is hardly necessary to add that that was
the end.[23] I have sometimes heard it suggested that
present-day Liberal statesmen tend, with the passage
of time, to become more and more like Mackenzie
King. It is interesting that King himself, as he grew
old, seems to have become more and more like Sir
John A. Macdonald.

In the last weeks of King's life the Korean War
broke out. On June 30, 1950, the ex-prime minister
recalled how he had blown up in the Cabinet in 1947
over a proposal that Canada should become a
member of a United Nations commission on Korea.
He wrote a final comment: "The more I think over
the whole situation, the more I believe, first of all,
that the U.S. foreign policy at bottom is to bring
Canada into as many situations affecting themselves
as possible with a view to leading ultimately to the
annexation of our two countries."[24]

In the end, we come back to the question of the
quintessential King, if there was such a creature.
What were his real views about the relationship of
his country to Britain and the United States?
Obviously, we are faced with a mass of contradic-

tions. How are we to reconcile his talk in 1935 about wanting to choose "the American road" if the Americans would let him, with his later apprehensions about American plans to absorb Canada? And many people have found it difficult to reconcile his declarations of devotion to the Commonwealth with his practical isolationism and refusal to accept Commonwealth commitments.

In fact, this strange man, who gets even stranger as one explores through his diaries the private life that his countrymen knew so little about when he was alive, makes pretty good sense politically — as, indeed, he needed to do to be the greatest vote-getter in Canadian history. As for his attitude to the United States, his long residence in that country and his many ties with it had merely served to strengthen in him the harmless superstitions about Canadian–American relations that were almost universal among Canadians of his time — superstitions centring on the hundred years of peace and the undefended border. His policies towards the United States were peace — which, like most Canadians, he took for granted — friendship, and, up to the limits of political discretion, free trade. That passing phrase of 1935, "the American road", I do not take too seriously. It was put into King's mouth by O. D. Skelton. At that moment King was desperately anxious to get a trade agreement, and no doubt he told the Americans what he thought they would like to hear. The words certainly did not represent King's conception of long-term national policy.

As for King's ideas and policies on relations with Britain and the Commonwealth, they are likely to be viewed with a more sympathetic eye today than they often were in the twenties and thirties. He inherited from Sir Wilfrid Laurier the concept of the Empire not as a nation but a league of nations, a community in which each nation's government and parliament retained full and unfettered autonomy. With that concept the future lay. The project of a unified Commonwealth foreign policy, based on consultation between the countries of the Commonwealth, which Borden and Christie believed in and which King and Skelton rejected and destroyed, was a noble experiment; but I question whether it could have had more than a temporary success. When one examines the Imperial Conference of 1921 and the Chanak Affair of the next year, one wonders whether it could have had even that.

There is no doubt at all, I think, that King sincerely believed in what he called in 1923 "a permanent imperial relationship" (he was slow to take up the word "Commonwealth"). Freedom within that larger association, and certainly not absorption into the United States, was the destiny of Canada as he saw it. I do not find him making much use of the word "independence"; perhaps he didn't like it, perhaps he thought it politically dangerous. It was, of course, easy to say that he paid lip-service to the Commonwealth while recognizing no practical obligations to it. In the background, however, lay the greatest obligation of all. He kept his mouth tightly shut about it in public, but clearly he could not conceive of Canada attempting to be neutral in a great war in which Britain was involved. As the Second World War approached, he avoided any "commitments", in the interest of maintaining national unity; but once the guns were actually firing, he and his cabinet recognized that national unity could be maintained only by participation.

Even O. D. Skelton had recognized a year before that this would be necessary.[25]

I said in my last lecture that Skelton, King's henchman, was an extreme Canadian nationalist who disliked British influences in Canadian life and policy and would have been glad to see them reduced and replaced by influences from the United States. King too was a nationalist (show me an eminent Canadian political leader who hasn't been) and, like Skelton, an isolationist; but he was less extreme in both respects and his emphases were different. His inherited preferences were for Britain rather than the United States. As the war approached, there was a certain tension between the two men, Skelton seeking to influence the prime minister against British policy, King tending increasingly to move towards Commonwealth solidarity. King, I think, was listening to ancestral voices (not from the spirit world, but from his inheritance). After war began, King reviewed his pre-war speeches and regretted that he had not gone further in following his own impulses and "stating [the] probability of war and of Canada's probable part in any conflict that related to aggression". The best parts of the speeches, he decided, were those he had put in in the face of "strong protest" from "S. and others at the office".[26]

Finally, I think that we must take note of a distinct paranoid streak in Mackenzie King. He worried about plots. There were plots by Tories to centralize the Empire (the most extreme case I know of was in 1914, when, for one moment, King seemed prepared to accept the proposition that the First World War was all a Tory plot to subvert Canadian autonomy). We have seen that during and after the

Second World War he became convinced that "the Americans" were plotting to take over Canada. And it may be recalled that on at least one occasion, in 1944, he suddenly decided that some of his own cabinet colleagues were plotting against him, a revelation that led him to dismiss Colonel Ralston.[27]

In the last case, it seems clear that there was, in fact, no plot, and I am afraid we must conclude that there were probably no plots in the other cases either. The fact is that King, like all good Canadians, thought that Canada was the centre of the world. His reason must have told him that Canada was in fact a very small object on both the British and the American horizons, but he found it hard to accept this in practice. The further fact is that the vast majority of British politicians were not sufficiently interested in Canada, or even in the Dominions as a whole, to bother with plotting about them. Ignorance and apathy were the real problems. The British government collectively became aware of the Dominions only when some sudden crisis recalled them to mind, as in the case of Chanak, when an attempt was made to throw them into the Mediterranean power balance with dire results. It is instructive to read the volume of the authorized biography of Winston Churchill which deals with those years after the First World War.[28] Churchill was Colonial Secretary, and had the heavy tasks of dealing with Palestine, Mesopotamia, and, in practice, Ireland; in all three he acquitted himself well. But his biographer shows no comprehension at all of the fact that in those same years the Commonwealth — Britain and the Dominions — was at a crucial turning-point; and we must assume that Churchill himself had no comprehension of it either. In King's first years as prime minister the British minister responsible for Commonwealth relations had no particular interest in the Dominions and — literally — no time for them. This explains a good deal.

As for the Americans, it is surely hard to take quite seriously King's belief at the end of his life that it was an object of United States foreign policy to bring about the annexation of Canada. (Can this have been an echo from his Victorian youth?) He must have forgotten — what he certainly knew in his younger days — how excruciatingly uninterested in Canada Americans are. In any list of the goals of American policy, the acquisition of Canada would surely stand very low indeed. The salvation of Canadian independence, I have always suspected, has been the facts, first, that so few Americans have any interest in Canada; secondly, that so few of those who have any interest are interested in taking us over; and thirdly, that those who might like to take us over are all convinced that union will ultimately take place without any overt action on their part — for who would not be an American if he could?

The modern problems of Canadian–American relations do not stem from plotting by the United States government. There is very heavy cultural pressure which is the result of the impact of modern capitalism and technology on the relationship of an enormously wealthy and populous country with a much smaller and weaker neighbour. And there is very heavy economic pressure which results from the desire of powerful individuals and corporations to make a fast buck — a great many fast bucks. These menaces are more subtle and more complicated, and in many ways much more difficult to deal with, than the mere hostility of a government. King was aware of the economic problem, but not so much, I think, of the cultural one.

At the end of his career, Mackenzie King's view of his country's situation was fairly pessimistic. In 1946, in one of the passages where he declared his belief that it was American policy to absorb Canada, he made it clear that in his view the decline of Britain's position in the world had made Canada's position more uncomfortable. Perhaps absorption was coming: "It might be inevitable for us to have to submit to it — being so few in numbers and no longer able to look to British power for protection."[29] What he would do if faced with our present situation no one can say. I think there were some respects in which he misapprehended the country's problems. But I should not be altogether surprised if he turned up, one of these days, as the patron saint of the new nationalism.

REFERENCES

Notes consisting merely of dates are references to the Mackenzie King Diaries.

MACKENZIE KING'S PERSONAL ATLANTIC TRIANGLE

1. February 8, 1902.
2. June 1, 1943.
3. J. W. Pickersgill & D. F. Forster, *The Mackenzie King Record*, 4 vols. (Toronto, 1960-1970), Vol. 1, 194.
4. *Ibid.*, Vol. 2, 433.
5. C. P. Stacey, *A Very Double Life: The Private World of Mackenzie King* (Toronto, 1976), 112-15.
6. March 13, 1949.
7. House of Commons, April 20, 1920.
8. F. A. McGregor, *The Fall & Rise of Mackenzie King: 1911-1919* (Toronto, 1962), 272 (Diary, November 23, 1918).
9. Diary, Mission to the Orient, December 15, 1909 [1908].
10. *A Very Double Life,* 137, 185.
11. October 14 and 26, 1899; January 31, 1901.
12. *A Very Double Life,* 171-73.
13. December 17, 1934, and memorandum of sitting, "Laurier House, Dec. 17, 1934", attached to

original diary. In this case, King's description and commentary in the diary text is more detailed than the memorandum.

14. April 18, 1934.
15. *A Very Double Life,* 157–58, 179–80.
16. Diary, Mission to the Orient, December 1908. The visit to Fallodon was on December 28–29.
17. July 31 to August 3, 1914.
18. Memoranda of séances, January 6, 1934 [1935], January 13, 1935, October 6 and 13, 1935.
19. *A Very Double Life,* 209–14.
20. May 27, 1934.
21. November 20, 1947.

THE HERMIT KINGDOM 1921–1930

1. Oxford, 1929, 128.
2. February 18–22, 1919.
3. *Mackenzie King Record,* Vol. 2, 87 (Diary, September 16, 1944).
4. Oscar Douglas Skelton, *Life and Letters of Sir Wilfrid Laurier,* 2 vols. (Toronto, 1921), Vol. 2, 293 (1902).
5. September 14, 1930.
6. *What's Past is Prologue: The Memoirs of the Right Honourable Vincent Massey, C. H.* (Toronto, 1963), 135.
7. March 18 and September 11, 1929, November 14, 1938. On the 1938 reference, see J. L. Granatstein and Robert Bothwell, " 'A Self-Evident National Duty': Canadian Foreign Pol-

icy, 1935–1939", *Journal of Imperial and Commonwealth History,* January 1975.

8. Skelton to Shortt, March 1902, Shortt Papers, Queen's University. I owe this reference to the kindness of Norman Hillmer.

9. James Eayrs, *In Defence of Canada: From the Great War to the Great Depression* (Toronto, [1964]), 71-80. C. P. Stacey, *Arms, Men and Governments: The War Policies of Canada, 1939–1945* (Ottawa, 1970), 95.

10. September 27, 1920.

11. *In Defence of Canada,* 162–65.

12. C. P. Stacey, ed., *The Arts of War and Peace,* Historical Documents of Canada, Vol. 5 (Toronto, 1972), 522-23. Diary, January 11, 1923.

13. December 20, 1928.

14. *Arms, Men and Governments,* 485-86.

15. January 22, 1924.

16. R. MacGregor Dawson, *William Lyon Mackenzie King: A Political Biography, 1874–1923* (Toronto, 1958), 409.

17. C. P. Stacey, "From Meighen to King: The Reversal of Canadian External Policies, 1921-1923", *Transactions of the Royal Society of Canada,* 1969. *The Arts of War and Peace,* 431-51.

18. Memorandum by Borden, January 20, 1919, R. A. MacKay, ed., *Documents on Canadian External Relations,* Vol. 2, *The Paris Peace Conference of 1919* (Ottawa, 1969), 30-31.

19. *The Arts of War and Peace,* 437.

20. *Ibid.,* 424-31.

21. King's Conference Diary, October 17, 1923.

22. *Ibid.*, October 20, 1923.
23. August 4, 1927. Keith Middlemas and John Barnes, *Baldwin: A Biography* (London, 1969), mention a visit by Lucy Baldwin to a fortune-teller in 1919 (72).
24. August 4, 1927.
25. July 30, August 4, 1927.
26. January 18, 1911.
27. *Globe,* Toronto, July 13, 1922.
28. *Ibid.*, July 13 and 14, 1922.
29. To Sec. of State for Colonies from the Governor General, "for Prime Minister from my Prime Minister", August 8, 1922 (King Papers, Public Archives of Canada, J1, Vol. 81, folios 68610-15).
30. Public Record Office, London, C.O. 42/1041 (microfilm reel B 3368, P.A.C.), minute by E. J. H. Harding, August 10, 1922.
31. Draft, *Ibid.*, reel B 3369. King's cable to Lloyd George, and the reply, dated October 19, 1922, are in a Canadian confidential print, King Papers, MG26, J4, Vol. 58, Memoranda and Notes, No. 370.
32. *Robert Laird Borden, His Memoirs,* 2 vols. (Toronto, 1938), Vol. 2, 769-73.
33. Lovell C. Clark, ed., *Documents on Canadian External Relations,* Vol. 3, (Ottawa, 1970), 898-915.
34. November 17, 1922.

THE JUNIOR PARTNER 1935-1948

1. Stacey, *A Very Double Life,* 183-84 and Figure 21.
2. *Dana Wilgress Memoirs* (Toronto, 1967), 100-02.
3. *Foreign Relations of the United States: Diplomatic Papers, 1935,* Vol. 2 (Washington, 1952), 27-30. C. P. Stacey, "The Turning-Point: Canadian-American Relations during the Roosevelt-King Era", *Canada, An Historical Magazine,* Autumn 1973.
4. November 8, 1935.
5. Stacey, *Arms, Men and Governments,* 327-38.
6. *Ibid.,* 341.
7. August 15, 1929.
8. *Arms, Men and Governments,* 98-9. Pickersgill and Forster, *Mackenzie King Record,* Vol. 1, 32.
9. Personal telegrams, King to Chamberlain and to Churchill, May 10, 1940, King Papers, P.A.C. (these were loose papers when I consulted them). King to Churchill, May 20, 1940, *ibid.*
10. November 25, 1947.
11. *Mackenzie King Record,* Vol. 1, 576-77; Vol. 4, 36 *ff.*
12. *The Arts of War and Peace,* 121.
13. *Mike: The Memoirs of the Right Honourable Lester B. Pearson,* Vol. 1 (Toronto, 1972), 215.
14. January 12, 1948.
15. *Arms, Men and Governments,* 154.
16. *Mike,* 1, 215.
17. July 19, 1943. Cf. *The Mackenzie King Record,* Vol. 1, 527-28.
18. July 24, 1943. *The Arts of War and Peace,* 608.

19. *Mackenzie King Record,* Vol. 1, 528.
20. *Arms, Men and Governments,* 185-87.
21. G. W. L. Nicholson, *The Canadians in Italy* (Ottawa, 1956), 73-75.
22. *Arms, Men and Governments,* 384-88.
23. *Mackenzie King Record,* Vol. 4, 259-73.
24. *A Very Double Life,* 219.
25. *Arms, Men and Governments,* 7.
26. January 14, 1940.
27. August 3, 1914. *Arms, Men and Governments,* 441-60.
28. Martin Gilbert, *Winston S. Churchill,* Vol. 4: 1916–1922 (London, 1975).
29. *Mackenzie King Record,* Vol. 3, 219.